KICKBOXING

MARTIAL AND FIGHTING ARTS SERIES

Judo

Jujutsu

Karate

Kickboxing

Kung Fu

Martial Arts for Athletic Conditioning

Martial Arts for Children

Martial Arts for the Mind

Martial Arts for People with Disabilities

Martial Arts for Special Forces

Martial Arts for Women

Ninjutsu

Taekwondo

KICKBOXING

NATHAN JOHNSON

Senior Consultant Editor
Aidan Trimble (6th Dan)
Former World, European, and
British Karate Champion
Chairman and Chief Instructor to the
Federation of Shotokan Karate

MASON CREST PUBLISHERS
www.masoncrest.com

Mason Crest Publishers Inc.
370 Reed Road
Broomall, PA, 19008
(866) MCP-BOOK (toll free)
www.masoncrest.com

First printing

1 2 3 4 5 6 7 8 9 10

Library of Congress Cataloging-in-Publication Data on file at the Library of Congress

ISBN 1-59084-392-4

Editorial and design by
Amber Books Ltd.
Bradley's Close
74–77 White Lion Street
London N1 9PF
www.amberbooks.co.uk

Project Editor Chris Stone
Design www.stylus-design.com
Picture Research Lisa Wren

Color reproduction by MRM Graphics, England
Printed and bound in Jordan

IMPORTANT NOTICE
The techniques and information described in this publication are for use in dire circumstances only where the safety of the individual is at risk. Accordingly, the publisher and copyright owner cannot accept any responsibility for any prosecution or proceedings brought or instituted against any person or body as a result of the use or misuse of the techniques and information within.

Picture Credits
Paul Clifton: 6, 11, 12, 18, 30, 35, 37, 62, 70, 77, 79, 80.
Nathan Johnson: 32, 39, 52, 54, 59, 64, 67, 69.
Sporting Pictures: 17, 61, 74.
Bob Willingham: 8, 56, 82.

Front cover image: Paul Clifton

Contents

Introduction

When I began studying the martial arts back in 1972, the whole subject was shrouded in mystery; indeed, that was part of the attraction. At that time there was only a limited range of books on the subject and therefore very little information was available to the novice.

I am glad to say that this has changed in recent years beyond all recognition. With the explosion of interest in the martial arts and the vast array of quality books that are now on the market, we seem to be increasing our knowledge and understanding of the martial arts and sports science, and this fact is reflected in this new series of books.

Over the past 30 years, I have been privileged to compete, train, and teach with practitioners from most of the disciplines covered in this series. I have coached world champions, developed and adapted training methods for people with disabilities, and instructed members of the armed forces in close-quarter techniques. I can warmly recommend this series as a rich source of information for students and instructors alike. Books can never replace a good instructor and club, but the student who does not study when the training is finished will never progress.

Aidan Trimble—Sixth Dan, Former World Karate Champion

The airborne kick is a favorite crowd pleaser and a good point scorer. The kicker must be in perfect control of his or her takeoff and landing, as he or she will be vulnerable to a counterattack when he or she lands.

Boxing with Kicks

Although street fighting has always had its own rules (or, more accurately, lack of rules), if we were to go back only a couple of generations in the West, we would find that kicking was not considered to be gentlemanly in a fight. Today, virtually every movie or television fight scene that lasts more than a few seconds involves kicking techniques.

Indeed, the present generation of movie-goers and martial artists expect to see kicking techniques in fights. Kicking techniques also form the basis for the martial arts movements shown in video games, illustrated in comic books, and written in books about the martial arts.

There are so many different martial arts that an accurate classification of them would be impossible. Even within a given tradition, techniques and training procedures vary from club to club and from group to group. Many martial arts, including the most modern ones, were undoubtedly inspired by martial arts from China and Japan. This includes the modern art of kickboxing. Martial arts are commonly used for entertainment purposes, but true martial arts involve much more than flashy demonstrations; their creation was for more serious reasons, such as self-defense and personal

Not all kicking techniques are thrown with deadly intentions. Sometimes, kicks are thrown lightly, particularly to help a training partner work on his or her defenses.

discipline. Martial arts can be practiced by people of all ages. Training takes many forms, and can be tailored to suit differing levels of fitness and ability.

Kickboxing is a modern martial art as well as a sport. It was created by combining Western and Thai boxing techniques with other techniques drawn from a variety of more traditional Oriental martial arts, including kung fu, karate, and taekwondo.

Kung fu is a Cantonese word that can be roughly translated as "hard work." But kung fu is a really a vulgar expression for an older term, **wu-shu**. Wu-shu is comprised of two Chinese characters (ideograms): wu and shu, meaning, "to stop or quell a spear." The term "wu-shu" thus describes a Chinese form of martial art.

Karate is a Japanese word for a martial art that uses blocking, punching, striking, kicking, seizing, grappling, and throwing techniques. Karate is written using two kanji, or Japanese characters (ideograms): kara and te. Kara means "empty," and te means "hand," or "hands." The word "karate" is therefore translated as "the art of empty hands" or "the art of fighting without weapons."

Taekwondo is a Korean martial art that is, likely, based largely on Japanese and Okinawan karate. Taekwondo favors high kicks, free-**sparring** techniques, and sporting contests. In fact, modern taekwondo is an Olympic sport.

Kickboxing was established during the martial art boom of the 1970s. More eclectic and free, and far less formal than traditional Oriental martial arts, kickboxing really took off in the U.S. and the U.K., where some of the first freestyle groups were developed and established.

Unlike more conservative and traditional martial arts, kickboxing places

The American kickboxing supremos Bill "Superfoot" Wallace and Joe Lewis "eye" each other up—tongue-in-cheek fashion. Lewis and Wallace spearheaded American kickboxing. Having been hook-punched by Bill, I can vouch for why he is so successful!

no emphasis on set movements, forms, or **kata** (traditional sole choreographed sequences of movements). It is largely independent from Oriental philosophy, as well as Eastern codes of behavior and healing techniques (although Thai boxers—the Eastern form of kickboxers—do have their health monitored when they are competing).

Some claim that American karate tournament fighters became frustrated with the tournament scoring system and devised kickboxing as a full-contact alternative. In fact, kickboxing has only a few similarities to karate—and then only to a certain type of karate, called **bogu kumite**. The

Benny "The Jet" Urquidez doing a (very) high front kick. Everyone tried to beat him and failed! Benny still draws huge crowds—particularly among his American and Japanese fans, even though he is retired.

similarities between kickboxing and bogu kumite include the use of protective equipment and full-contact blows and kicks. There are many differences between the two, however, and one of the biggest can be found in the hand techniques. While bogu kumite uses karate punching techniques, modern kickboxing uses Western boxing techniques, including jabs, hooks, crosses, uppercuts, and a wide range of other types of body blows.

In kickboxing, great emphasis is placed on delivering punches with full force, as is done in boxing proper. Because early kickboxing had a poor reputation for safety, the World Kickboxing Association and other regulating bodies were set up during the 1970s. Early kickboxing superstars from this era included the incomparable Joe Lewis, Bill "Superfoot" Wallis, and the unforgettable Benny "The Jet" Urquidez, possibly the most successful kickboxer ever.

Martial artists are renowned for being able to defend themselves with nothing more than their bare hands. This means that they must learn to transform fists, elbows, knees, and feet into a range of practical, natural weapons. Kickboxers—perhaps even more so than other martial artists— need to cultivate extremely practical techniques because, ultimately, they may be tested in the kickboxing ring.

THAI BOXING

Thai boxing is a unique form of boxing that includes kicking techniques, grabbing and holding techniques, and tripping and sweeping techniques. There are many similarities between Eastern kickboxing methods, such as Thai boxing, and Western kickboxing methods.

Specialty Thai boxing methods include the roundhouse kick and an extensive use of elbow and knee techniques. The elbow point and the flat of the elbow are used at close quarters to strike upwards, downwards, backwards, and horizontally. The knee is used at both long and medium ranges, as well as at close quarters. The following are some examples of Thai boxing knee techniques.

DIAGONAL KNEE STRIKE

Seizing your opponent at close quarters, grapple with him or her by grabbing his or her neck. Pulling his or her head forward onto your shoulder, execute a diagonal knee strike to your opponent's solar plexus.

FLYING KNEE STRIKE

This is an especially spectacular Thai boxing technique. Leap off the ground and lunge towards your opponent's solar plexus, chest, or head with an extended knee. Take care to protect your head when using this technique, or you may be struck while advancing.

RISING KNEE STRIKE

Your opponent has attempted a right hook. Leaning back to avoid the attack, throw forward your right hand, grasp the back of your opponent's neck, and pull him or her forward onto a rising knee strike.

THE HISTORY OF THAI BOXING

The ancestors of the Thai people originally came from China. These early settlers were driven south into the Mekong and Salween valleys during the

KNEE STRIKES

FLYING KNEE STRIKE: Keep well guarded while airborne to minimize the danger of counterattack.

RISING KNEE STRIKE: This tactic is a favorite of Thai boxers who use it with brutal efficiency.

13th century. There, they mixed with the **indigenous** Khmer population.

It is hard to find any genuine traditional connection between early warfare in Thailand and the art of Thai boxing. Early Thai battles were fought between armies of **infantry** equipped with shields and helmets, and the introduction of firearms during the 16th century made many of the existing military strategies and tactics obsolete.

Thai boxing proper seems to have been cultivated in and around the social life associated with Thai religious temples. Because Thai boxing hand techniques closely resemble Western boxing techniques, it is difficult to believe that Western boxing techniques were a later invention.

Ancient Thailand did possess a form of ritualized combat: a weapons system known as **krabbee-krabong**, or "sword-spear." The krabbee was a short, single-edged, curved blade. Krabbee-krabong fighters also used a round shield for protection. The combat was choreographed, but the sheer speed and ferocity of the techniques survived the centuries, and krabbee-krabong can still be seen as a martial art.

At the beginning of the 20th century, Thai boxing was taught in Siamese schools. The number of injuries sustained in training was high, however, and so the government was forced to put a stop to it. Nevertheless, Thai boxing continued to flourish, and today it can be found all over Thailand, especially in Bangkok.

Early Thai boxing was a bloody and violent affair, with no weight divisions or proper rules (although biting, hair pulling, and kicking a fallen opponent were forbidden). Thai boxing only took up the use of boxing gloves in 1929. In earlier times, fighters used to bind their hands and forearms with horsehide strips. Later, this binding was replaced with a rope made from hemp (a coarse, rope-like grass) or glue-soaked strips of cotton. According to some sources, some fighters even mixed ground glass into their bindings.

MODERN THAI BOXING

Modern Thai boxing, although more refined, is still a grueling business, and it is common for professional Thai boxers to train for five hours or more per day. Training is so severe and contests so punishing, that the life

Even though there are rules in Thai boxing and kickboxing, contests can be punishing. Here, a kickboxer successfully blocks a round kick with a combination of a raised knee and a protective forearm cover/block.

expectancy of serious Thai boxers is considerably reduced, and a Thai boxer's career typically does not last more than six years or so. It is common for a Thai boxer to take as his **surname** the name of the camp in which he trains, to show his loyalty.

Many Thai boxers train twice a day: once in the morning and once in the afternoon. Thai boxers training for a fight undergo a medical and weight check on the morning of the fight. The fighters usually receive a long massage before the fight with special sports oil called namman muay,

Kickboxing has become popular with women. Here, two young women clash—one uses a lead hand hook punch and the other a lead leg round kick—probably kickboxing's most distinctive kick.

which is used to increase blood circulation and to improve and enhance muscular performance.

All fights are accompanied by loud, and sometimes menacing and discordant, music. Although absent from modern Western kickboxing, ritual plays an important role in Thai boxing. Before stepping into the ring, a boxer will kneel down, often with his or her teacher, and engage in a short prayer. The boxer will then kneel and face the direction of his or her training camp, home, or birthplace, cover his or her eyes with his or her gloved hands, and bow low, touching the canvas three times in salutation.

Following this prayer, the boxer will perform a ritual dance called **ram muay** that consists of a slow shadow-boxing routine. The boxer may move around, stopping at each corner of the ring, where he or she may lower his or her head and stamp his or her foot several times to assert his or her dominance. This routine serves as a warm-up exercise, and is also a form of mental preparation.

Many Thai boxers wear a piece of cloth containing a protective charm around one upper arm. This cloth is called **kruang rang**. A boxer may also wear a piece of "sacred cord," called a **mongkol**, which belongs to his or her teacher or trainer. This cord is removed before the fight. Thai boxing fights are usually scheduled for five three-minute rounds with two one-minute breaks in between.

Thai boxers engage in fitness and stamina training. This training includes long-distance running, as well as handheld focus and punching and kicking pads. The training techniques for which Thai boxers are most famous, however, are the shin-toughening and pounding drills. Thai boxers toughen their shins by impacting them on bottles filled with sand and by kicking

A TOURIST ATTRACTION

Although Thai boxing is international, it is currently seen as the national Thai sport, and is a popular tourist attraction. Public events staged for tourists tend not to feature the current top competitors; rather, they feature former champions and older boxers, who finish the twilight of their careers at these popular (but less prestigious) events.

hanging bags filled with a variety of materials. Impacting their shins on these surfaces is designed to desensitize them to pain. These practices should not be attempted without supervision, however, as they can be extremely painful and disfiguring.

KICKING TECHNIQUES

Foot techniques expand the arsenal of natural weapons found in Thai boxing and kickboxing. Natural weapons on the foot include the ball of the foot, the top of the arch, the little toe edge of the foot, and the heel. Like its Western counterpart, kickboxing, Thai boxing has also borrowed techniques from Western boxing, kung fu, karate, and taekwondo, but one characteristic feature of Thai boxing is its distinctive and much-used roundhouse kick.

THE ROUNDHOUSE KICK

The roundhouse kick is a type of kick in which the body pivots, using the non-kicking leg as an axis. This kick differs from those found in other types

THE ROUNDHOUSE KICK

STEP 1: Starting from a stable base, smoothly begin to swing your leg forward.

STEP 2: Arc your leg up and out in the beginnings of a semicircle.

STEP 3: Ensure that you keep your guard up when landing the kick.

THE BENEFITS OF KICKBOXING

Kickboxing offers many benefits to those who practice it. The following list is by no means exhaustive:

- Increases confidence
- Increases fitness, strength, and flexibility
- Improves stamina
- Provides a measure of self-defense

of martial arts because contact is made with the shin. The kick is delivered primarily by a twisting action of the body, and thus the leg need not be primed to the same extent as is necessary for a karate kick. The kicking leg is held almost straight on delivery.

To perform this kick, raise your knee, lift it out to the side, and then bring it forward and across your body. Pivot the supporting leg outwards, keeping the raised leg relaxed. Continue pivoting the supporting leg until it has turned more than 90 degrees. Keeping both elbows tucked into your ribs and your chin down (to avoid any counterattack), lean your body away from the target, and then arc the kick into the target, striking with the shin.

THE FRONT KICK

The front kick is the most manageable kick to perform. Raise the knee of your kicking leg so that it is at least parallel with the floor. Make sure that the knee of the supporting, or platform, leg is well bent and that the supporting foot is pointing forward. Thrust the kicking leg out and forward while pushing the ankle forward and pulling the toes back, so that if the kick were to land, it would make contact with the ball of the foot.

THE SIDE KICK

Raise the knee of your kicking leg so that it is at least parallel with the floor. Make sure that the knee of the supporting, or platform, leg is well bent and

THE FRONT KICK

Make sure you avoid "telegraphing" (letting your opponent see the kick coming). Aim the kick by pointing the knee at the target. The kick is landed using the ball of the foot as an impact point.

that the supporting foot is pointing sideways. Turn your hips until the thigh of the kicking leg faces the intended target and the lead hip is in a comfortable position. Thrust the kicking leg sideways and out while bending the ankle and pulling the toes back. The point of contact is the edge of the foot.

THE ROUND KICK

Raise the knee of your kicking leg so that it is at least parallel with the floor. Make sure that the knee of the supporting, or platform, leg is well bent and that the supporting foot is pointing sideways. Begin to turn the hip of the kicking leg as you "flick" the leg out in a semicircle.

The point of contact for this kick should be either the top of the arch or the ball of the foot.

THE BACK KICK

Pivoting on the ball of your front leg, turn your body 180 degrees. Raise the knee of your kicking leg so that it is at least parallel with the floor. Make sure that the knee of the supporting, or platform, leg is well bent and that the supporting foot is pointing directly backwards. Thrust the kicking leg out backwards, towards the target.

The point of contact for this kick should be the heel.

THE JUMPING KICK

Raise the knee of the rear leg so that the thigh is parallel with the floor. Spring off the ground with the front leg, then flick out a front kick with the rear leg, followed swiftly by a mid-air front kick with the front leg.

THE SIDE KICK

Thrust the side kick to your intended target, taking care to position your hips properly. The side kick, although appearing in several martial arts, is executed with subtle differences. For example, the side snap kick, which is quickly retracted, and the side thrust kick, which is delivered with a follow-through.

There are other kicks in the kickboxing repertoire, including the spinning kick, the flying side kick, the flying round kick, and the jumping-back-spinning kick. Although such kicks are popular for demonstrations, they are considered impractical for real fighting.

THE ROUND KICK

STEP 1: Make sure that the toes of the supporting leg are turned out and away from your intended target.

STEP 2: After full extension, prepare to withdraw the kicking leg as quickly as possible to avoid getting caught by a counterattack.

WESTERN KICKBOXING

There are two basic types of modern Western kickboxing: **semi-contact**, in which the combatants are only allowed to land light, controlled blows; and **full-contact**, in which the ultimate aim is to achieve a knockout. Individual schools and clubs hold interclub open or invitation competitions and engage in both national and international competitions.

Although both men and women practice kickboxing, the two sexes do not compete against each other. Combat rules differ between the various organizations, and most authorities are extremely wary of injuries. Both men and women are expected to wear protective equipment, including head guards; gum shields; shin, hand, and foot pads; and groin guards for men and chest guards for women. Western kickboxing and Thai boxing differ in this regard, as Thai boxers normally only wear boxing gloves, groin guards, and gum shields.

Western kickboxing also differs from Thai boxing in that it makes greater use of both karate- and taekwondo-type kicking techniques. This is particularly true of semi-contact kickboxing. Indeed, it is not uncommon for semi-contact kickboxers to wear modern karate-style uniforms tied with a traditional karate belt (called an obi).

SAFETY AND KICKING TECHNIQUES

When performing the kicking techniques of any martial art, it is important to remember that some people are naturally more flexible than others. People who are less flexible risk injury if they try to copy those who are more naturally flexible. In order to keep kicks safe, keep them as natural as possible.

THE BACK KICK

STEP 1: Turn to face the target quickly, but carefully. Do not strain turning your head!

STEP 2: Kick outwards and backwards as naturally as you can. Turn your body to face your target as soon as you have completed the kick.

In addition, pay particular attention to the knee and hip positions during the preparatory stages of a kick, particularly when executing side and round kicks. It is easy to develop strains if you are not properly warmed up.

The most effective kicks are those that are kept within the individual's natural range of movement. With practice, this range of movement can be successfully extended. However, if it is overextended, damage—or even serious injury, such as groin strain or a hernia—can result, so be careful.

THE JUMPING KICK

STEP 1: Kick forward with a middle-level front kick.

STEP 2: Launch yourself strongly into the air and prepare to extend a second kick quickly.

STEP 3: Take care to keep impact with the floor to a minimum to protect the knee joint.

Kickboxing for Fitness and Fun

Modern kickboxing is used by a number of fitness clubs as a means to work out, stay in shape, and have fun. At such clubs, the confrontational or combative elements of kickboxing are reduced, and some clubs even go so far as to remove contact sparring altogether.

Kickboxing can be fun if the fitness element is stressed. You can practice the various techniques alone, in shadow-boxing fashion, or you can practice a kind of "mock sparring" with a partner, in which well-controlled (almost slow-motion) techniques are thrown, but with absolutely no contact.

The image of kickboxing has changed recently, from a sort of "spit and sawdust," nitty-gritty affair (mostly practiced by men) to a more accessible and popular recreational activity practiced by men, women, and children. Kickboxing clubs have now opened up in most major cities. Some of these clubs are open to the public, while others are private, such as college and university clubs. Private coaching is also available, with some personal fitness coaches adding kickboxing to fitness regimes constructed for individuals.

Kickboxing has become a Westernized synthesis of many existing martial arts, yet it retains its own unique character. As martial arts go, it is fluid,

There is little exotic or esoteric theory in kickboxing. Techniques either work, or they do not. The impact power of this front kick can be "felt" by the person holding the pad.

informal, and short on theory—particularly when compared to the esoteric types found in some other martial arts. Despite this lack of sophistication, however, kickboxing remains effective—even brutally so—and realistic in both its outlook and the practical results to come from hard, serious training.

WARMING UP

Before you can practice kickboxing, you will need to warm up. You should work towards the goal of strengthening and toning your body to keep fit

Unlike Western boxing, Thai boxing permits (encourages!) holding and hitting. In this example, a female kickboxer controls her opponent with a neck-hold as she lands a knee strike to his solar plexus.

A ROYAL ENDORSEMENT

Kickboxing was given a boost in the U.K. when a popular member of the royal family went public with the fact that she attended and enjoyed kickboxing classes. In fact, at one university in the U.K., the kickboxing club enrolled more members than any other martial arts club. The club also had a larger proportion of female members than any other martial arts club.

and to minimize the risk of injury during training. Following are some effective exercises for warming up.

ABDOMINAL CRUNCH

Lie comfortably on the floor, raise your knees, and place your hands at the sides of your head. Raise your body as you pull your knees up towards your

ABDOMINAL CRUNCH

Avoid doing this exercise on a full stomach. Do not try to do too may repetitions in the beginning. Start with a few and gradually work your way up.

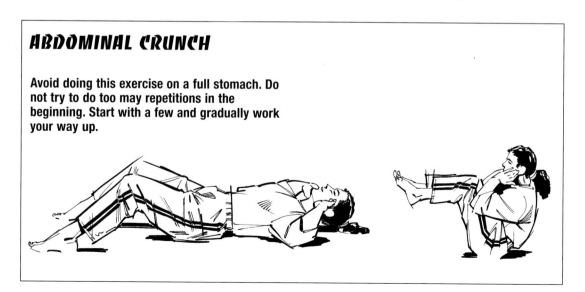

HORSE STANCE AND PUNCH

Punching outwards ad forward is a "loan" exercise borrowed from karate and taekwondo in the early days of kickboxing.

HAMSTRING STRETCH

As with all stretching and warm-up exercises, do not overdo the number of repetitions in the early stages of training.

chest, then lie back down, making sure that neither your feet nor your head touch the ground. Repeat several times.

HORSE STANCE AND PUNCH

Squat in a "horseback riding" stance by stretching your legs apart, keeping your back straight, and bending your knees. Thrust out alternately with your fists, holding each position for at least 30 seconds. Repeat several times.

HAMSTRING STRETCH

This exercise should be performed slowly and gently. It is designed to stretch and strengthen your hamstrings. It is important that you do not favor one leg over the other when doing this exercise.

Great flexibility is an asset in the ability to deliver kicking techniques, but remember, in a contest, you are statistically more likely to get knocked down or out by a punch.

ABDOMINAL PRESS

This exercise should be practiced with great care. Pay particular attention to spasms or twinges in your back. If you get any, do the exercise without a partner.

Have a training partner take hold of your leg at the ankle (ask him or her to avoid putting pressure on the tendon in your heel). Your partner should squat so that you can safely place your leg on his or her shoulder, and then he or she should carefully help you stretch your leg, which you should keep straight. Try to hold the position for a minimum of six seconds, and repeat several times on each leg.

ASSISTED ABDOMINAL CRUNCH

Lie on your back, and place your hands at the sides of your body or lightly on your stomach. Spreading your legs, slow your breathing and ask your partner to gently push down on your legs towards the floor (to stretch them

Landing blows on a moving target is the ultimate "litmus test" in kickboxing. You can, however, get a pretty good idea of the destructive power of your kicks by using a kicking bag. Here, a Thai boxer lands a high round kick.

for you) for 20 to 30 seconds. Repeat several times. It is important to perform this exercise carefully and to not push the legs down with great force.

ABDOMINAL PRESS

This exercise is designed to strengthen your stomach muscles. Lie on your back, and tuck your knees into your chest. Place your hands on the floor at your sides. Your partner should lean forward, resting on the soles of your feet, so there is a degree of tension between both of you. Hold this position for 10 to 20 seconds, making sure that it is not painful. Repeat several times.

TRAINING EQUIPMENT

Kickboxers make extensive use of equipment to practice focusing their blows. Training equipment includes kicking bags, punching bags, **focus mitts**, air shields, and speedballs.

Many types of martial arts use punching and kicking bags to help them perfect techniques. Traditional martial arts stylists often train to perfect their form by practicing techniques in the air. Modern kickboxers and full-contact fighters, however, typically spend considerable amounts of time hitting and kicking a variety of bags.

PUNCHING BAG

Punching bags are filled with a variety of different materials and range in firmness. If you are going to hit a punching bag repeatedly and powerfully with your fists, you should wear special gloves designed for this purpose. Consider having your hands bandaged prior to a heavy workout with a bag.

When you go to hit a punching bag for the first time, you will most likely get a shock—your blows will probably slip and glance off the bag. It takes skill and experience to land a solid jab punch like this.

Bandaging the hands is an old boxing safety measure designed to prevent "knuckle spread," a condition in which the base joints of the fingers become loosened and spread out as a result of repeated impact on a bag. If you are going to kick a bag, it needs to be heavy enough to provide resistance, but soft enough not to damage your legs, even after repeated impact.

Punching bags are used to develop a full range of punching techniques, including jab, cross, hook, and uppercut punches.

THE JAB PUNCH

When throwing a jab punch, the lead arm is thrust out and forward, corkscrewing or spiraling as it goes (the arm is never fully extended,

JAB PUNCH

STEP 1: Adopt a ready stance, watching and waiting for the right moment to throw the punch.

STEP 2: Throw out the jab and be ready to retract it the instant it lands. Make sure the returning hand is held up to protect your chin.

however). When performing this punch, take care to slightly raise the shoulder of the punching arm; keep the chin tucked in and the guard hand (the non-punching hand) held high, with the elbow protecting the ribs. These defensive measures offer protection against a counterattack, particularly a hook to the head. This punch is thrown from medium to long range. Targets for the jab punch include the chin, the nose, and the eyes.

CROSS PUNCH

When throwing the cross punch, be prepared to receive a counterpunch, unless you score cleanly.

THE CROSS PUNCH

This is a powerful punch that is thrown diagonally, usually using your strongest arm. It is often used in combination with the jab punch. Like the jab punch, it is thrown from medium to long range.

To throw a cross punch, thrust out the punching arm from one side of your body, so that the punch crosses an imaginary midline. When using the cross punch, be sure to keep the non-punching hand upright, with the elbow pointing down to protect the ribs and the fist near (but not touching) the jaw to protect it.

The target of this punch is usually an opponent's jaw. One of the effects of this punch is a knockout.

HOOK PUNCH

STEP 1: From a well-guarded position, prepare to "power out" a hook punch.

STEP 2: You may choose to exhale forcefully when you execute this punch. It definitely adds to the powered focus.

THE HOOK PUNCH

This is a short-power punch thrown from close range. It can be thrown with either the lead or the rear hand. To throw this punch, begin by thrusting the punching arm out and forward. After this initial movement, raise the elbow, tighten the shoulder and armpit, and land the punch with a horizontal hooking action, with the back of the knuckles facing upwards.

Delivered in a horizontal arc, this type of punch is devastating if it lands on a target with considerable force. The power of this punch derives from the fact that it is "shortened," which means that less power escapes from the elbow of the punching arm. Moreover, one theory says that the human body produces the most power through a natural curve movement (such as the one in this punch). This theory, however, runs contrary to that of modern karate, which says that the most power is produced using a straight trajectory.

THE UPPERCUT PUNCH

Like the hook punch, this is a short punch delivered from close range. Sometimes, however, it is used in an extended form as a type of "sucker" punch as a surprise-attack tactic to catch an opponent unaware.

Uppercut punches can be thrown with the lead or the rear hand. To throw this punch, arc the punching hand upward

UPPERCUT PUNCH

This picture illustrates an uppercut thrown with the rear hand. It is one of the most devastating punches in the kickboxing arsenal.

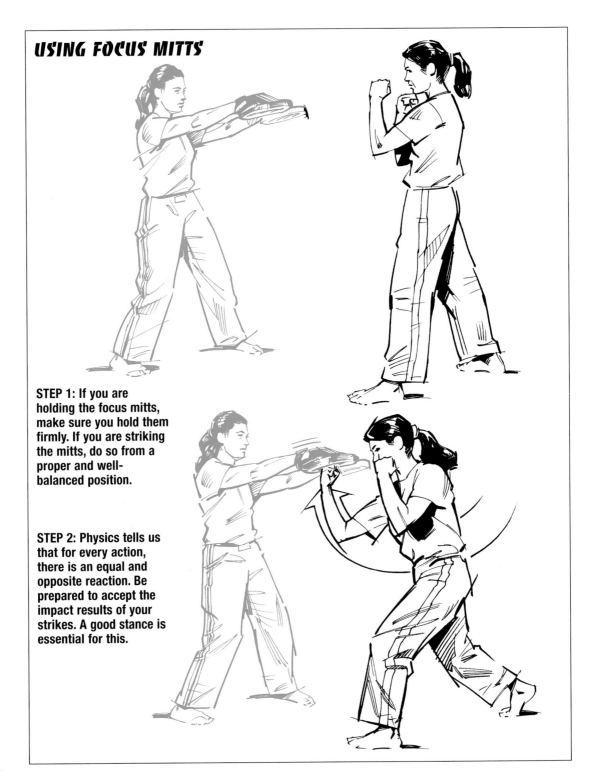

USING FOCUS MITTS

STEP 1: If you are holding the focus mitts, make sure you hold them firmly. If you are striking the mitts, do so from a proper and well-balanced position.

STEP 2: Physics tells us that for every action, there is an equal and opposite reaction. Be prepared to accept the impact results of your strikes. A good stance is essential for this.

with a crouching action. Make sure to keep the chin tucked in and the non-punching hand protecting the chin and ribs. The uppercut rises quickly from a low level to a high one. A well-thrown uppercut that snaps an opponent's head back (which frequently results in a knockout) is one of the most controversial aspects of kickboxing, Thai boxing, and Western boxing, because of the potential damage that can be caused by the punch.

FOCUS MITTS

Most modern martial arts, including kickboxing, use focus mitts. These mitts are used in conjunction with a partner in order to improve accuracy, timing, and speed. A partner holds the pads in a particular position to invite a specific technique. For example, he or she may hold the mitt pad-side to the ground to invite an uppercut punch to be thrown.

The basic angles at which the focus mitts are held are square on (for jabs), sideways (for turning kicks), and angled (for hooks). Reaction time can be improved by suddenly changing the position of the mitt so that you have to decide quickly which technique to use. Focus mitts can be used singularly or in pairs. Once you become competent at hitting a moving target with a high degree of accuracy, you will be able to put together combinations with blinding speed, a must for effective full-contact fighting.

Here is an effective practice technique using focus mitts. Have your partner stand just within your natural distance (about the length of your leg), holding either one or two focus mitts. Ask him or her to stand still at first, until you get used to landing a clean, focused blow on the mitt. Once you can do this, ask your partner to move around, changing distances while moving backwards, sideways, or even forward, to cramp your space.

USING THE KICKING BAG

Not all kickboxing is about sweat and pain. Experimenting with a kicking bag can be good and rewarding fun. And, you can find out for yourself how a particular technique works best for you! Thrust the round kick out strongly, making sure you do not bend your head forward; otherwise the impact might unbalance you.

Once your confidence and skill have increased, you could ask your training partner to launch partial attacks at you using the mitts. The purpose of these attacks is not to land a punch; they are just to provoke a reaction. Your partner might, for example, step forward and launch a light left-hooking action towards your head, completing the action by placing the focus mitt in a position that invites you to counter with a right cross punch.

KICKING BAGS

Kicking bags are filled with a variety of different materials and, like punching bags, vary in firmness from soft to hard. Typically, a more experienced practitioner would use a harder bag for training.

Two types of round kick, the Thai boxing round kick (see pp. 24 and 26) and the kickboxing round kick (see pp. 20–22), can be practiced using a kicking bag. When practicing the round kick using a kicking bag, make sure that you do not stand too close to the bag. Your supporting leg should be well bent and angled away from the bag.

Here is an effective practice technique using a kicking bag. Begin by kicking the bag lightly, performing no more than 10 kicks with each leg before changing sides. Gradually increase the pace and power of the kicks until they reach full power. Drop the pace down again after two to three minutes to allow accumulated toxins to filter out of the bloodstream (the after-burn of oxygen creates toxins that can give you a "stitch"). After a minute or so of slow tempo, increase your output to its maximum. Repeat the cycle according to your own level of fitness or according to your training program.

AIR SHIELDS

All of the blows and kicks that can be practiced using a kicking bag can also be practiced using an air shield. Air shields come in a variety of shapes and sizes, and are usually filled with foam. They can be used to develop focus, timing, rhythm, and power. Air shields differ considerably from focus mitts because they are capable of soaking up great impact force and will tax your power reserves.

Air shields come with a variety of handles and gripping devices, and it is important to learn how to hold them properly. Failure to do so will result in the impact of the blows causing the shield to hit the person holding it (usually somewhere unpleasant, like the face). Also, improperly held air shields will prevent the blows and kicks being practiced from landing properly (they tend to slide off the air shield if it is not held correctly).

Here is an effective practice technique using an air shield. Have a partner stand in front of you, presenting a properly held air shield. Practice one blow or kick at a time until you are skillful and confident enough to put a combination or series of combinations together.

SPEEDBALLS

The speedball is a piece of equipment borrowed from conventional boxing. It is a small, light, inflated ball about the size of a small melon. The ball is suspended at head height or just above. The speedball is used to develop rhythm, timing, and fluidity. Using the speedball has little to do with developing overall punching power, however, and is not struck with conventional blows.

Using a speedball will help you develop the muscles you need to keep your hands up during sparring or in tournament fighting. A kickboxer who lets his or her guard drop will usually be struck and knocked down or out, which is why it is vital to maintain a proper guard at all times. Using the speedball will help to cultivate and maintain this habit.

COMBINATIONS

STEP 1: Prime the knee by raising it as shown, to prepare for step 2.

STEP 2: Fully extend the leg in a round kick.

STEP 3: Follow the round kick with a jab punch.

STEP 4: Finish with a rear hand hook punch.

HOW TO STRIKE A SPEEDBALL

You will find using a speedball to be a bit tricky at first. The problem lies in trying to locate the speedball after it has bounced off the circular board from which it is suspended. With a bit of practice, however, you will get used to it.

Stand facing the speedball in a natural and relaxed posture. It is customary to advance the leg you would naturally put forward when

USING A SPEEDBALL

Rhythm, timing, speed, and eye-hand coordination are all enhanced by using a speedball.

shadow boxing, sparring, or using a punching bag. Raise your arms so that they are in front of the speedball, and clench your fists. An optional move now is to twist and spiral your left fist clockwise, and your right wrist counterclockwise (this twisting motion adds a preparatory "tone" to your forearms). Letting your wrists spring back from their twisted state (if you have twisted them), punch your fists towards the speedball, one after another, in rapid and rhythmic succession. Raise your elbows to work the muscles on the undersides of your arms (the triceps), while simultaneously working your shoulder muscles (the deltoids).

Speedball blows should be hit with a sort of a rolling, tumbling action, with the blows landing from above the ball.

A KICKBOXING FITNESS REGIME

The following kickboxing fitness regime is given merely as an example; fitness routines are most effective when they are tailored to suit an individual. The example is based on eight categories of training: calisthenics, stretching, kicking bag work, kicking in the air, skipping, boxing bag work, shadow boxing, and running.

CALISTHENICS

You should gradually increase the number of repetitions given for each exercise. Do not worry if your friends can do more push-ups than you can, as the training should be tailored to suit your own ability.

PUSH-UPS

Lie face down on the floor with your legs slightly apart. Place the palms of your hands flat on the floor with your arms placed slightly beyond the width of your shoulders. Raise your body upwards, until your arms are straight, and then gently lower yourself down until your body almost touches the ground (your lowered body may touch the ground so long as it does not bear any weight). Do not hold your breath during this exercise.

Start with as many repetitions as you can comfortably manage and progressively build up in sets of 8 to 10 repetitions. Please bear in mind that push-ups are not an indication of general strength and that some people can naturally do more than others. Each person should, therefore, concentrate on his or her own performance. Do 5 to 10 repetitions if you are new to this exercise.

SQUAT THRUSTS

Place the palms of your hands flat on the floor with your arms placed slightly beyond the width of your shoulders. Raise your body upwards until your arms are straight. Drive forward with your knees, tucking them in and up towards your chest while maintaining your arm and upper body position. To complete one action, thrust back with your legs until your feet are in their original position. This action should be done smoothly and

Running is part of many sports fitness regimes, particularly combat sports like kickboxing that have a competitive basis. Be sure to wear proper running shoes if you are running on concrete, otherwise stick to softer ground.

carefully to avoid strain or injury. Do 10 to 15 repetitions if you are new to this exercise.

JUMP-UPS

Begin by placing the palms of your hands flat on the floor with your arms slightly beyond the width of your shoulders. Raise your body upwards until your arms are straight. Drive forward with your knees, tucking them in and up towards your chest while maintaining your arm and upper-body position. Jump or stand up quickly from the crouching position. Do five repetitions if you are new to this exercise.

SIT-UPS

This exercise concentrates on tightening and strengthening the abdominal muscles. Good control of the abdominal muscles is vital in any martial art. Sit-ups also help to develop stamina.

Lie flat on your back, and bend your knees approximately 90 degrees. Have a partner hold your ankles. Raising your hands to the sides of your head and keeping your elbows tucked in, lift your body about 45 degrees from the floor while exhaling. Lower yourself down again as you inhale. Do 5 to 10 repetitions if you are new to this exercise.

STAR JUMPS

Starting in a natural and relaxed posture, throw your arms out and up as you jump up, spreading your legs as you do so. Jump up repeatedly, opening and closing your legs as you simultaneously throw your arms out and up to the sides.

Each generation of skilled combatants has something valuable to pass on to the next. Raw aggression will not overcome skill, power, and experience. Here, a young boxer receives cheerful advice about his right cross punch.

There is a risk of sustained injury if you overdo this exercise. Do only five repetitions if you are a beginner.

STRETCHING

Stretching should be done for 10 to 15 minutes. Some stretching exercises are detailed on pp. 32–38.

KICKING IN THE AIR

When practicing air-kicking techniques, you should concentrate on speed. As usual, make sure that you are properly warmed up. An effective practice regime is as follows: 15 to 20 repetitions of the round kick, the side kick, and the front kick.

SKIPPING

Using a skipping rope is a popular form of exercise for building a person's overall fitness, reflexes, and levels of endurance. It is a favored means of training for most boxers. To get the most from this technique, skip for two minutes, rest, and then repeat.

BOXING BAG WORK

Using a light focus pad, practice the following techniques for two minutes on both sides: jabs, hooks, crosses, and uppercuts.

SHADOW BOXING

To practice shadow boxing, simply go through the movements or techniques you have already learned, and try to incorporate new techniques, variations, and combinations. It is also good to vary the speed, combinations, timing, and rhythms used.

Avoid full extension of your limbs when shadow boxing, as fully locking the arms or legs when practicing techniques in the air may make your knee or elbow joints ache. Taken to the extreme, this can develop into "tennis elbow" (an inflammation of the elbow joint causing pain common to racket-based sports) or inflamed tendons. To avoid such injury, keep your

Wearing boxing gloves alters the natural clench of a fighter's grip, as the fist is not tightly clenched. This can occasionally lead to injury during contests. A fighter who suspects such an injury should stop the bout immediately.

CAUTION

If the brain is repeatedly damaged, the effects will multiply. In such a situation, a martial artist, like a boxer, may become "punch drunk" (slurred speech and impaired brain and reflex responses caused by receiving too many blows to the head). In semi-contact sparring, these risks are minimized; but because kickboxing techniques are so powerful, even a single poorly controlled kick to the head can cause serious injury, even in a semi-contact sparring situation.

movements fluid, do not fully extend your limbs, and keep your movements and techniques as natural as possible. Practice on both sides for two minutes each.

FULL-CONTACT FIGHTING

Full-contact is a general term that applies to karate, taekwondo, kung fu, Thai boxing, and kickboxing. Each has slightly different systems of competition; some are based on semi-contact fighting, whereas others are based on full-contact fighting.

In semi-contact fighting, kicks and punches are landed with controlled force at accepted targets, while in full-contact fighting, full-force blows and kicks are delivered. The most dangerous category of fighting is obviously full-contact because the risk of injury—particularly to the brain—is great.

The brain is a soft-tissue organ. Although the skull protects the brain in most circumstances, if the head is struck forcibly, the brain will suffer injury.

In fact, thousands of brain cells are destroyed every time the head is struck. The damage is not immediately obvious; somebody who has been repeatedly punched or kicked in the head may complain of a headache or suffer from poor concentration in the short term. So long as the damage is not serious, however, recovery can take place. Of course, the wearing of headguards will dramatically reduce the level of risk.

Full-contact fighting was devised as a way of allowing all of the impact-based martial arts to compete both against themselves and against each other. Initially, there appeared to be stylistic differences between certain types of martial arts fighters (kung fu fighters and karate or taekwondo fighters, for example), but these differences later disappeared as the fighters' experience grew, and they discovered what works and what does not work in the ring.

Surprisingly, traditional techniques were less effective in the full-contact ring than had been imagined. Kicks like the "back turning" or "spinning" kick, a great scoring technique in semi-contact fighting, proved to be woefully inadequate in full-contact fighting. Moreover, when the technique failed (as it invariably did), the kicker was often punished for being caught off-balance or with his or her back turned or with his or her head and body facing away from the point of conflict. The use of punching bags also changed opinions as to what would work and what would not work in the full-contact ring, as some blows and kicks proved to be more effective than others.

FOOTWORK

According to kickboxing superstar and former world heavyweight kickboxing champion Joe Lewis, footwork is the most important thing in

Natural instincts for self-preservation and survival are heightened during kickboxing sparring. Here, the intense concentration on the faces of these kickboxers demonstrates these enhanced instincts.

fighting and precedes everything. Once a kickboxer becomes quick on his or her feet, he or she can transfer this speed to punches and kicks, thereby making them powerful. Kickboxers without mobility are ineffective because they are unable to land their punches and kicks.

Kickboxers do not move in fixed patterns. Unlike karate and other related martial arts, kickboxing does not use a full step to deliver a punch. Effective

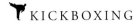

WINNING TIPS

There are no formal stances or positions in kickboxing. The key to good footwork is to keep mobile and keep covered. Do not let your hands dangle by your sides, even if you have seen boxers like Mohammad Ali or Sugar Ray Leonard do so. Keep your hands in a good guard position, and move on the balls of your feet. Finally, never stand flat-footed, or you may get caught by a combination.

kickboxing footwork should be as natural as possible. This means that you should move your body smoothly and quickly, keeping your balance and remaining light on your feet. Avoid dancing around unnecessarily. Also, never hold rigid or tense defensive positions, as these have a negative effect on the mind and will lead you to cower if you get hit. Nature provided the "fight-or-flight responses" (see p. 64). Use them.

BODY EVASION

Some kickboxers claim that the best defense is a good offense, but even this requires good positioning and the avoidance of an opponent's attack through body shifting or repositioning. Repositioning can best be understood in terms of the points of the compass. There are eight basic directions that can be taken—backwards, forwards, sideways (both ways), and any combination thereof.

Moving backwards is both natural and easy, but your opponent can continue moving forward—and can do so faster than you can move backwards. Moving sideways and backwards is an excellent tactic because it forces your opponent to readjust his or her position in order to follow you. Moving sideways and forwards is also effective, provided that you have good close-quarters skills and can neutralize any attacks. Even just going forward into an attack can be a form of evasion.

Finally, some fighters favor "tying up" another fighter's arms, entangling them and preventing the other fighter from launching a punching attack. This tactic is not quite as effective in kickboxing as it is in normal boxing, because a kickboxer can still use a leg technique, even in a "clinch."

Despite the long range of kicking techniques, and despite the legs being approximately four times stronger than the arms, some kickboxing tournaments have to stipulate that a minimum of eight kicks must be thrown per round, because it is often difficult to land clean kicks on a moving target.

Kickboxing as Self-Defense

While certain tactics can help boost your confidence, it is important not to have unrealistic expectations about what you can actually do to protect yourself in a situation—otherwise, you may find yourself in over your head. You must accurately and honestly weigh the given situation before deciding how to act.

There is a world of difference between the self-defense needs of a warrior on a battlefield and those of a child being picked on in the schoolyard. Consequently, a combat-active Marine will not receive the same training as, say, a young person taking kickboxing classes. Generally speaking, however, there are certain elements of self-defense that apply equally to all types of situations that call for it.

One of the best-known defenses of all time is already programmed into the human brain. It requires little training and is generally extremely effective. It is also a good recipe for a long life. It is called running away. Standing and fighting is something that should always be avoided unless you have no other choice.

Timing is a critical factor in the success of a kicking technique. In a tournament situation, it is quite common for both fighters to attempt to kick at the same time. When this happens, the fighter who is the quickest off the mark with a punching technique will be the most likely to score.

It is a mistake to be ashamed of being afraid. Fear is a natural reaction and can even be used in a positive way as part of the mental preparation for conflict. Under stress, our bodies produce a natural hormone called adrenaline. When we are faced with a challenging or threatening situation, adrenaline is pumped into the bloodstream to provide us with an energy boost. This reaction prepares us for what is known as the "fight-or-flight syndrome."

There are two consequences of fear that can affect us adversely. The first is that sometimes it can paralyze us, making us freeze and do nothing—sometimes with disastrous consequences. The second consequence of fear is that it can cause a drastic over-reaction.

We commonly experience the paralyzing type of fear in situations of general bullying, especially when the bullying happens within our peer group (among our classmates or colleagues, for example).

Good mental preparation is essential for success. A fighter should be relaxed—so as not to waste energy—and properly warmed up.

Virtually every school—and even every workplace—has its bully, and he or she comes in an astonishing variety of guises. Furthermore, there is both physical bullying and mental bullying. For the purposes of this book, however, we will concentrate on physical bullying.

Many people who bully others understand that what they are doing is wrong, but they still feel the need to bully for one reason: because they are afraid themselves. In simple terms, the bully's act of bullying others is an overreaction to his or her own fear. The bully cannot find his or her desired position or status within his or her peer group, which makes him or her afraid, and so he or she decides to impose the status that he or she wants.

Some bullies use force, while others torment their victims mentally. All bullies, however, impose their "high" status within their peer group by diminishing the position of others. In short, the bully's drive is based in insecurity. Often, the bully's downfall comes from his or her feelings of guilt about what he or she is doing.

Bullies choose their victims based on who they perceive to be weak. The victim usually has few friends (or perhaps no friends), no network, and no support system. This is exactly why the bully chooses them: because they have no one to support them against the bully. Such a victim offers no threat to the bully's actual (or desired) position.

DEALING WITH A BULLY

The question that we are faced with is how to deal with a bully on a practical level. If we stop and think about it, we find that the solution is actually rather simple: bullies need both a victim and an audience. If both are

INSIDE A BULLY'S HEAD

Bullies use certain tactics to achieve their bullying:
- They try to shock and impress the impressionable.
- Bullies usually demonstrate a certain "unreasonable ruthlessness" towards the victim. (The stronger members of the class or social group will not necessarily share this feeling.)
- They cater to the feelings of rebellion commonly experienced during adolescence.

removed, then clearly no bullying can take place. Granted, a victim can be bullied without an audience, but this only provides a short-term thrill for the bully, although it may be awful for the victim.

If a bully starts up with you, try not to put yourself in a position where you have to tackle him or her alone. Go for support. The more support, the better, particularly from the group that the bully has to live among. This obviously does not include any like-minded friends of the bully, but it does include teachers, parents, sports coaches, and "reasonable" members of his or her group of friends—even his or her relatives. Basically, anyone who is a part of the bully's community may be able to help.

IF YOU HAVE TO FIGHT

First and foremost, always try to avoid any fight in which a weapon is threatened. If you are caught in a situation in which a weapon is produced, you must keep away from it at all costs. Improvise a weapon of your own, if necessary, but remember that an attacker may take your improvised weapon as a greater threat and act even more unreasonably.

You must also take into consideration the attacker's distance, timing, and the nature of the weapon concerned. For example, if you are threatened

Children and young people can safely enjoy sparring only if they treat it as a game, and use their natural (play) instincts to control the distance—as they do in schoolyard games such as "tag."

DOUBLE COVER

When double covering, make sure that your fists do not obscure your line of vision.

with a knife and you pick up a chair to use as a weapon, you may be able to keep an attacker at bay over the long and middle ranges. At close range, however, the chair will be next to useless, and you would probably be wise to discard it.

Something else to remember is to always protect your head at all costs. If your head takes a direct hit of sufficient power, your whole body may go down—you may be knocked out. When covering up, guarding, or otherwise protecting yourself, keep your forearms tucked into your ribs, your shoulders up, and your chin tucked in. Turn in your front foot to bring your front thigh in and towards your groin to protect it. Be prepared to punch your aggressor with all the force, training, and experience at your disposal. Take care to keep properly covered up while executing your punch, and never stop looking for an opportunity to escape.

Kickboxers need to control natural instincts—like aggression—and channel them into explosive combinations and skillful defenses.

Once you have delivered a punch, be prepared to follow up. A blistering combination should be able to beat someone of your own size and strength who has little or no experience fighting, even if he or she is a bully.

PHYSICAL PREPARATION

It is important to bear in mind that while punching someone will no doubt be unpleasant for him or her, it will likewise be painful for you. You will be making contact using your (unprotected) knuckles, and thus you should expect to incur some sort of injury. Practicing punching using a heavy punching bag can at least prepare you for the impact. Indeed, sports science tells us that the best way to warm up for an activity is to approximate that activity as closely as possible.

High kicks are seldom used as finishing techniques, but when an opening presents itself, they make spectacular finishing techniques.

It is only through constant repetition that the skills of defense and offense can be learned, sharpened, and maintained. Basic skills can be acquired in a matter of months, and reflexes can be sharpened. It is important, however, to keep it all in perspective. Remember that no one can prepare for every eventuality. It would be unwise for you to fill your head with constant thoughts about a fight that may never happen.

In modern kickboxing, preemptive striking (hitting first) is always seriously considered. But hitting someone before they hit you does raise certain moral and ethical questions. For instance, how can you be sure that the person is really going to hit you? And even if you are relatively sure that the person is going to hit you, how do you know how hard the blow will be? It could be just a light blow that you could either tolerate or quickly escape from after it was delivered. Would the blow deserve the devastating combination that you are about to unleash on your opponent?

The final decision regarding preemptive striking rests with you, but if you can avoid it in any way, you should do so. It is always best to wait for the other person to strike out first and then defend yourself and hit back, if necessary. Also, bear in mind that if you hit someone else first, you could get into trouble with the law.

DEFENDING YOURSELF

In training to defend yourself using kickboxing, what is required is a measure of realism. In order to benefit from the training described in the following paragraphs, you will need a competent partner or trainer. You will also need appropriate equipment. This will consist of a gum shield, a head guard, a body protector, and two pairs of boxing gloves.

The idea in self-defense kickboxing training is to familiarize yourself with being physically assaulted. Facing one blow at a time is fairly simple and will instill basic confidence; however, things get trickier when facing a **compound attack**.

A compound attack is an attack consisting of an unspecified number of blows, delivered in fierce combinations that cover the full range of

GETTING CAUGHT BY A PUNCH

STEP 1: When your opponent is close enough to be able to hit you, you should be properly covered—unlike this example.

STEP 2: And remember, your opponent's lead (front) hand is the closest to you and can reach you quickly…ouch!

kickboxing techniques. Starting with a single attack (preferably by a trusty friend or an experienced coach), gradually build up the number of attacks, until you can defend yourself against a compound attack. There are a number of techniques that can be used to absorb this type of punishment without getting hurt.

One problem with a compound attack, however, is that when defending against one, you will start to become anxious and will likely try to predict what type of attack is coming next. It is vital to curtail this habit.

Do not try to "block" each and every individual technique. Keep covered instead. Protect your jaws with your fist and your ribs with your elbows. Move your body continually in order to avoid becoming a "sitting duck." Roll with the punches, and slide back, sideways, or even forward to avoid or check kicks. Duck, bob, and weave, and be prepared to explode with a dynamic compound combination of your own when you sense an opening.

Using the double-cover guard in which both arms protect you from blows to an area from the jaw to the ribs, pivot, twist, duck, roll, and dodge to avoid a compound attack. You could also consider moving forward and inward in order to stifle attacks at the source. If you do so, however, be prepared to use short punching techniques (hooks or uppercuts, for example) to counterattack.

In training to absorb and neutralize blows in this way, you will gain valuable defensive skills that only kickboxing training can provide. You will also gain the useful experience of following up a defensive position with an immediate counterattack, which is, arguably, the most important tactic in any martial art.

ROLLING WITH THE PUNCHES

STEP 1: Keep well covered, pivot, twist, and roll when you are attacked with a compound attack (many blows).

STEP 2: Be prepared to "spring out" from the double defensive guard with a counter-attack.

Applied Kickboxing

There is a recent phenomenon in the world of kickboxing called kyokushinkai karate. Unlike more-conventional karate, kyokushinkai karate is characterized by a fierce, contact knockdown fighting system that is similar to full-contact kickboxing.

Korean-born Masutatsu Oyama developed **kyokushinkai karate** after the Second World War. Kyokushinkai fighters have a worldwide reputation for toughness, and the style has an international organization with many thousands of members. A popular karate style, kyokushinkai karate has captured the imaginations of two generations, and incredibly, there are over 23 published biographies of its charismatic founder.

Part of the success story of kyokushinkai karate was due to Oyama's energetic promotion of his brand of karate throughout the world. During the 1960s, he toured the U.S. and other countries giving spectacular demonstrations. These demonstrations included wood-breaking techniques, as well as the smashing of rocks, stones, bricks, tiles, and huge slabs of ice using punches, karate chops, knee, elbow, and shin strikes, and even head butts! Kyokushinkai **karate-ka** (someone who practices karate) also chopped

The quickest person off the mark does not always win. Just like the old Wild West days, accuracy is vital, particularly in the use of kicking techniques. They can leave a fighter vulnerable if they miss.

the necks off standing beer bottles and smashed airborne melons with punches and spear finger strikes. Another trick was to punch or kick out the flame of a candle.

Masutatsu Oyama was a legend during his lifetime, and stories about his exploits still circulate. By today's standards, his behavior might seem radical or extreme; however, he was very much a product of the time and the environment in which he lived (post-Second World War Japan). Controversially, he had himself been filmed fighting bulls barehanded (film footage showed the bull to be rather small, however). Oyama also secluded himself on a mountainside, allegedly shaving off an eyebrow to prevent himself from returning to civilization during a moment of weakness.

ONE HUNDRED-MAN KUMITE

Oyama will always be remembered for his development of the "100-man kumite." "Kumite" is a Japanese word consisting of two parts: kumi and te. Kumi means "meeting," and te means "hand." The word "kumite" thus refers to sparring, and the "100-man kumite" refers to one man having 100 consecutive full-contact **bouts**. It is a challenge of strength, endurance, and above all, survival.

Kyokushinkai full-contact bouts are no light matter. Kicks are permitted to the head; the hands are carried high; and it seems that none of the participants have ever heard of protective equipment. A fighter who gets knocked down for more than five seconds fails the challenge, even if the knockdown occurs in the last fight. To make matters even more difficult, in order to succeed, a fighter must win a greater percentage of

Thai boxing is well known for the relentless and ferocious use it makes of low kicks aimed particularly at the supporting leg of a kicking opponent.

A KYOKUSHINKAI KNOCKDOWN FULL-CONTACT THIGH KICK

As your opponent moves towards you, sidestep the attack and counter with a round kick to your opponent's thigh. Be prepared to follow up with a punching combination.

fights by scoring **ippon** (full, clean point-scoring techniques). Moreover, a fighter must not employ delaying tactics just to stay in the fight.

It will come as no surprise, given the described conditions, that few people have been successful in the 100-man kumite. A fighter who succeeds does so entirely with his or her own physical ability. The test takes over three hours. Each fighter must compete with full commitment and aggression.

The original rules were simple: bare-hand punches to the face and kicks to the joints were allowed.

Three "greats" who successfully participated in the 100-man kumite test were Shihan Steve Arneil (May 21, 1965), Shihan Tadashi Nakamura (October 15, 1965), and Shihan Shigeru Oyama (September 17, 1966). (The title **Shihan** is used to recognize one of the highest grades of master.) These three masters rigorously prepared for their kumite by stretching, running, skipping, bag work, basics, and free fighting. Totally committed, they spent most of each day in the training hall (called the **dojo**) for months.

Preparation times for the 100-man kumite test varied. Originally, the candidates were not told when the test would take place. For example, when Britain's Steve Arneil was preparing for the test, he turned up early for what he thought was an ordinary Sunday training session and noticed that the changing room was empty. Normally, it would have been crowded and bustling with students.

Changing into his uniform (called a gi), Arneil made his way

The legendary Steve Morris, who is graded to 3rd dan by the esteemed Gogen "The Cat" Yamaguchi, seen here striking a hanging bag.

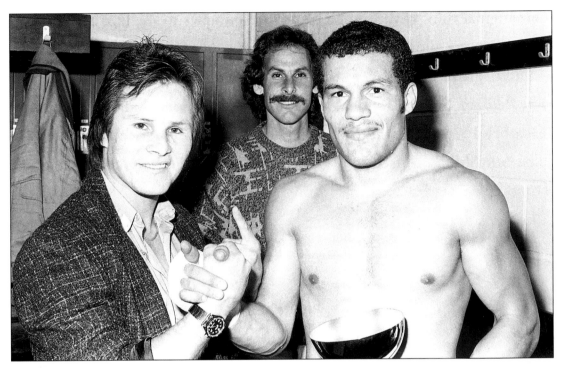

The legendary Benny "The Jet" Urquidez (left) offers congratulations to a young fighter. Kickboxing is one of the toughest sports in the world to stay at the top of.

to the hall in time for class. Upon entering the dojo, he found it crowded with his fellow karate-ka. Oyama approached Arneil and informed him that "the time had come" and that the test was at hand. Arneil stood in the center of the dojo, surrounded by karate-ka, and the dojo drum was struck once, as a signal for the first fight to commence.

Arneil did not actually knock anyone out, although he did knock down many of his opponents during the three hours of gruelling, non-stop fighting. He was knocked down a few times himself, too, but he always got to his feet and started fighting again, unassisted and within the set time. Steve Arneil completed the 100-man kumite and made karate history. At the time of this writing, he is still active in karate and has trained many thousands of karate students in a career spanning more than 40 years.

SPARRING

A kickboxer's main goal is to improve practical fighting skills. Philosophical considerations are secondary to this objective, and all other exercises (running, weight training, and the use of equipment) are merely supportive. The key to improving fighting is a form of practice fighting called "sparring." It is only during sparring that the fighter gets to experience the unpredictability of an opponent.

The amount of sparring conducted in a given training session is determined by the purpose of the training; that is, whether the fighter is preparing for a tournament, or whether he or she is merely in routine training. If a fighter is preparing for a tournament, most of his or her workout should consist of sparring and equipment training. For general training, more time can be given to stamina, flexibility, and running—even to weight-training drills.

It is useful to approach sparring by breaking it down into techniques. A series of progressive sparring drills is outlined in the following paragraphs.

SINGLE-TECHNIQUE SPARRING

Single-technique sparring concentrates on practicing only one technique. In this type of sparring, fighters take turns at using a single technique. For example, you might throw a jab, which your partner might block and then throw a single technique back at you. This is a "tit-for-tat" practice that allows both practitioners a simple means of avoiding or blocking an

Body armor helps to soak up the power of otherwise-punishing body blows. Despite being best known for his 60-mph (96-km/h) side kick, Bill "Superfoot" Wallace destroyed many of his opponents with sound body blows.

attack and then counter-attacking.

This approach should not be confused with the prearranged "one-step" sparring of karate, in which the target is announced. In single-technique sparring, each person is allowed to spontaneously throw whichever technique he or she likes. In short, during single-technique sparring, students can move around freely, choose the moment to attack or defend, and select the target of their choice.

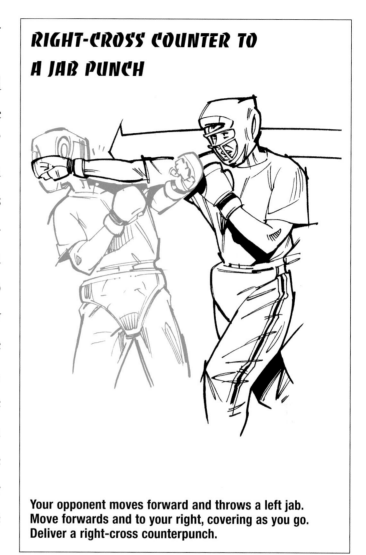

RIGHT-CROSS COUNTER TO A JAB PUNCH

Your opponent moves forward and throws a left jab. Move forwards and to your right, covering as you go. Deliver a right-cross counterpunch.

DOUBLE-TECHNIQUE SPARRING

Double-technique sparring builds on single-technique sparring (see previous section) and introduces the element of combination. The advantages of this type of practice include breaking a partner's concentration by "hitting high to score low" with the second technique—for instance, feigning a high target strike, ultimately to score a point

HOOK PUNCH, BODY PUNCH COUNTER AGAINST A JAB PUNCH

STEP 1: Your opponent leads with a left jab. Cover up, and counter with a right-hook punch that your opponent blocks.

STEP 2: Bounce off the block, and deliver a left hook to your opponent's body.

by hitting a low one. The student can also combine a leg technique with a hand technique.

TRIPLE-TECHNIQUE SPARRING

Triple-technique sparring is interesting because it challenges both the physical and mental abilities of the fighter. It produces its own particular rhythm, which is often difficult to deal with in sparring. World-class semi-contact fighters, like America's Kevin Brewerton and Britain's Jeff Thomson, achieved great success using this technique during the 1980s.

The secret to this type of sparring is based on a certain logic. The mind responds to one technique, is divided by two techniques, and is confused by three techniques. When using the triple-technique method, you can change the angle, height, or type of technique twice, thereby increasing your chances of scoring (you usually score with the third technique).

Triple-technique sparring differs from single- and double-technique sparring because here, you initiate the action, becoming offensive rather than defensive. A typical triple-sparring exchange might go something like this. You move forward with a left jab, which is blocked by your opponent. You then follow up with a right cross as a prelude to launching a left uppercut punch.

When using this technique, try to establish a broken rhythm (for instance, one, two...one, or one...one, two). A broken rhythm tends to surprise and confuse an opponent. If he or she gets used to a broken rhythm, however, you may find it more effective to use a regular rhythm. Experiment to find what works best for you.

CROSS, UPPERCUT COMBINATION

STEP 1: First deliver a right-cross punch to the side of your opponent's head.

STEP 2: Shorten the distance and deliver a sharp left uppercut, making sure you keep covered with your right hand.

FREE-SPARRING DRILL

A beginner observing free sparring for the first time might marvel at how the fighters know what to do and when to do it. Kicks, punches, evasions, **feints**, counterattacks, and **parries** all seem to be executed with skill and precision. This can only occur between two skilled fighters who know how to control their aggression, select their targets safely, and give each other space and opportunity. This type of sparring should not be confused with tournament fighting or with self-defense.

SEMI-CONTACT SPARRING DRILL

In this semi-contact sparring drill, contact should consist only of a strong tap. Special emphasis should be placed on avoiding injury to the face and groin areas.

Semi-contact sparring should be used as a bridge to full-contact sparring. It should never be allowed to degenerate into a free-for-all. Its purpose is to progressively improve your skills, not to "get one over" on your partner.

CONTROLLED FULL-CONTACT FIGHTING

One consistent theme of this book has been safety, and this applies particularly to full-contact fighting. Remember that your training partner is not a real opponent; you must learn to distinguish between him or her and someone who poses a genuine threat, either in the kickboxing ring or in a self-defense situation. The following are some permissible targets in full-contact fighting.

Controlled full-contact fighting is a modification of full-contact fighting proper. Correctly applied, it can lead you one step closer to all-out fighting.

SEMI-CONTACT SPARRING COMBINATION

The following type of combination can be effective, but you must be prepared to vary it depending on the circumstances. Move forward and attack with left middle-level side kick, close the distance, and deliver a right-hook punch. Keep covered up during the combination.

In this type of sparring, you are permitted to strike the trunk of your opponent's body, but not the face or the lower body. Sparring in this controlled manner allows the attacker to experience the consequences of landing his or her blows in terms of maintaining balance afterwards.

In the initial stages, only punches should be used. You should then progress to using only kicks, and finally, to using kicks and punches in combination.

FULL-CONTACT SPARRING

At this level of training, protective equipment is essential because you will now direct attacks towards your partner's face using leg and hand techniques.

Drills can be constructed for more extreme approaches to kickboxing. Such drills would include grabbing, holding, hitting, foot-sweeping (to trip

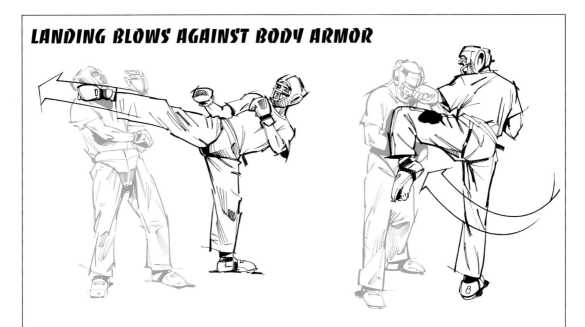

LANDING BLOWS AGAINST BODY ARMOR

The head, seen here attacked with a kick. Be aware when using a kicking technique to the head that your foot is the farthest weapon away. Remember as well that in full-contact fighting, you risk losing your balance if the kicking technique does not connect well, and that you will also be vulnerable to a speedy counterattack.

The trunk, seen here attacked with a knee. This technique is more typical of Thai boxing than of kickboxing. The general rule with the knee strike is to make sure that you have good contact with—or good control of—an opponent's arms or posture before using it.

your partner), and wresting or holding. Although not strictly speaking kickboxing, some modern styles have redefined themselves by using such techniques in combination with kickboxing proper. One example of this is called shoot fighting, which incorporates elements of kickboxing and other martial arts. In addition to the techniques described, shoot fighting also includes ground fighting and holding techniques.

FOOT-SWEEPING TECHNIQUES

Although commonly used in a variety of martial arts, this technique can be quite dangerous. The knee and ankle joints (the targets that suffer as a result of foot-sweeping attempts) are relatively weak and are extremely susceptible to injury. Injury to either of these joints often plagues martial artists, who sustain them for the rest of their lives. Furthermore, because the balance of a person being foot-swept is so profoundly disturbed, he or she is also at risk of fracturing elbows, shoulder blades, or suffering a concussion after falling badly.

The risks of using foot-sweeps are not limited to the potential damage suffered by an opponent. As an attacker using foot-sweep techniques, you risk damaging your own foot, ankle, or shin. In short, be careful when using this technique, and gain experience only by carefully prearranging its use.

FOOT-SWEEP AND TAKEDOWN COMBINATION

STEP 1: As your opponent slides forward to deliver a jab punch, slide your left leg behind and into his or her advancing leg.

STEP 2: Then hook and sweep his or her leg up and sideways. This will unbalance your attacker and make him or her fall.

Glossary

Bogu kumite karate	Early Japanese full-contact karate
Bout	An athletic match
Compound attack	An attack that combines several different moves
Dojo	A Japanese term used to describe the martial arts training hall
Feint	A pretend blow or attack on or toward one area in order to distract attention from the point one really intends to attack
Focus mitt	A pad used in training to help a kickboxer learn to aim his or her punches and kicks
Full-contact	Sparring or fighting in which full-powered blows are allowed to connect
Indigenous	Originating in a particular region or environment
Infantry	Soldiers trained, armed, and equipped to fight on foot
Ippon	One point or score
Karate-ka	A person who practices karate
Kata	Choreographed sequence of martial arts movements
Krabbee-krabong	A sword-, spear-, and shield-based martial art from Thailand
Kruang rang	A piece of cloth containing a protective charm worn by Thai boxers

Kyokushinkai karate	A type of Japanese knockdown, full-contact karate
Mongkol	A piece of "sacred" cord belonging to a Thai boxing teacher or trainer and worn by a fighter
Parry	To evade or ward off a weapon or a blow
Ram muay	A ritual dance conducted by Thai boxers before a fight
Semi-contact	Sparring or fighting in which light blows are allowed to connect
Shihan	A Japanese term used to recognize one of the highest grades of martial arts, that of master
Spar	To practice fighting
Surname	A person's last name
Wu-shu	This means "to stop or quell a spear."

Clothing and Equipment

CLOTHING

Gi: The gi is the most typical martial arts "uniform." Usually in white, but also available in other colors, it consists of a cotton thigh-length jacket and calf-length trousers. Gis come in three weights: light, medium, and heavy. Lightweight gis are cooler than heavyweight gis, but not as strong. The jacket is usually bound at the waist with a belt.

Belt: Belts are used in the martial arts to denote the rank and experience of the wearer. They are made from strong linen or cotton and wrap several times around the body before tying. Beginners usually wear a white belt, and the final belt is almost always black.

Hakama: A long folded skirt with five pleats at the front and one at the back. It is a traditional form of clothing in kendo, iaido, and jujutsu.

WEAPONS

Bokken: A bokken is a long wooden sword made from Japanese oak. Bokken are roughly the same size and shape as a traditional Japanese sword (katana).

Jo: The jo is a simple wooden staff about 4–5 ft (1.3–1.6 m) long and is a traditional weapon of karate and aikido.

Kamma: Two short-handled sickles used as a fighting tool in some types of karate and jujutsu.

Tanto: A wooden knife used for training purposes.

Hojo jutsu: A long rope with a noose on one end used in jujutsu to restrain attackers.

Sai: Long, thin, and sharp spikes, held like knives and featuring wide, spiked handguards just above the handles.

Tonfa: Short poles featuring side handles, like modern-day police batons.

Katana: A traditional Japanese sword with a slightly curved blade and a single, razor-sharp cutting edge.

Butterfly knives: A pair of knives, each one with a wide blade. They are used mainly in kung fu.

Shinai: A bamboo training sword used in the martial art of kendo.

Iaito: A stainless-steel training sword with a blunt blade used in the sword-based martial art of iaido.

TRAINING AIDS

Mook yan jong: A wooden dummy against which the martial artist practices his blocks and punches and conditions his limbs for combat.

Makiwara: A plank of wood set in the ground used for punching and kicking practice.

Focus pads: Circular pads worn on the hands by one person, while his or her partner uses the pads for training accurate punching.

PROTECTIVE EQUIPMENT

Headguard: A padded, protective helmet that protects the wearer from blows to the face and head.

Joint supports: Tight foam or bandage sleeves that go around elbow, knee, or ankle joints and protect the muscles and joints against damage during training.

Groin protector: A well-padded undergarment for men that protects the testicles and the abdomen from kicks and low punches.

Practice mitts: Lightweight boxing gloves that protect the wearer's hands from damage in sparring, and reduce the risk of cuts being inflicted on the opponent.

Chest protector: A sturdy shield worn by women over the chest to protect the breasts during sparring.

Further Reading

Baltazzi, Evan S. *Kickboxing: Safe Sport, Deadly Defense*. Boston: Charles E. Tuttle Co, 1976.

Boykin, Chad. *Muay Thai Kickboxing: The Ultimate Guide to Conditioning, Training, and Fighting*. Boulder, CO: Paladin Press, 2002.

Cave, Eddie. *Kickboxing*. New York: The Lyons Press, 2001.

Fox, Joe. *Kickboxing Basics*. New York: Sterling Publications, 1998.

Mezger, Guy. *The Complete Idiot's Guide to Kickboxing*. Indianapolis: Alpha Books, 2000.

Rochford, Tim. *Kickboxing Fitness*. San Diego: American Council on Exercise, 2000.

Sipe, Daniel. *Kickboxing: The Modern Martial Art* (Action Sports). Minneapolis: Capstone Books, 1994.

Urquidez, Benny. *Practical Kick-Boxing: Strategy in Training and Technique*. Los Angeles: Pro Action Publishing, 1982.

Useful Web Sites

http://martialarts.org/

http://www.uskba.com/

http://www.kickboxing.com/

http://www.wmto.org/

http://www.kickboxing-wka.co.uk/

http://www.kickboxing.net/

http://www.americankickboxing.com/

http://www.wklkickboxing.com/

About the Author

Nathan Johnson holds a 6th-dan black belt in karate and a 4th-degree black sash in traditional Chinese kung fu. He has studied martial arts for 30 years and holds seminars and lectures on martial arts and related subjects throughout the world. He teaches zen shorindo karate at several leading universities in the U.K. His previous books include *Zen Shaolin Karate* and *Barefoot Zen.* He lives in Hampshire, England.

Index

References in italics refer to illustration captions